The
WAR
of
Leadership

HARD LESSONS AND PRACTICAL TRUTHS FOR
SURVIVING IN AND BEYOND LEADERSHIP

Other works by

J. JASON HICKS

Fiction

Ruinwaster's Bane:
The Annals of the Last Emissary
Book One

The Earthmight War:
The Annals of the Last Emissary
Book Two

Curious about Jason's epic high fantasy series? Explore options to purchase Books One and Two from the Annals of the Last Emissary via this QR code:

The
WAR
of
Leadership

HARD LESSONS AND PRACTICAL TRUTHS FOR
SURVIVING IN AND BEYOND LEADERSHIP

J. Jason Hicks

ILLUSTRATIONS BY
VICTOR JUHASZ

Copyright © 2026 by J. Jason Hicks | jjasonhicks.com

All rights reserved. No portion of this book may be reproduced in any form without written permission from the publisher or author, except as permitted by U. S. copyright law.

No generative artificial intelligence (AI) was used in the writing of this work or art. The author reserves the rights for this work and contracted use of illustrations, which cannot be reproduced and/or otherwise used in any manner. The author expressly prohibits any entity from using this publication for purposes of training AI technologies to generate text or artwork, including, without limitation, technologies that are capable of generating works in the same style or genre as this publication.

Without limiting the rights under the copyright reserved above, no part of this publication may be reproduced, stored in or introduced into a retrieval system, or transmitted, in any form or by any means (electronic, mechanical, photocopying, recording, or otherwise), without the prior written permission of the copyright owner, publisher, and illustrator of this book.

The scanning, uploading, and distribution of this book via the Internet or via any other means without the permission of the publisher is illegal and punishable by law. Please purchase only authorized electronic editions and do not participate in or encourage electronic piracy of copyrightable materials. Your support of the author's rights is appreciated.

This publication is designed to provide accurate and authoritative information in regard to the subject matter covered. It is sold with the understanding that neither the author nor the publisher is engaged in rendering legal or other professional services. The advice and strategies contained herein may not be suitable for your situation. You should consult with a professional when appropriate. Neither the publisher nor author shall be liable for any loss of profit or any other commercial damages, including but not limited to special, incidental, consequential, personal, or other damages.

This is a work of nonfiction. All incidents in this book are either products of the author's imagination or used in a fictitious manner. Any resemblance to actual persons, living or dead, or actual events is purely coincidental.

For information about this title or to order other books
and/or electronic media, contact the publisher:

Dasmurwil Properties LLC
Tucson, Arizona USA
jjasonhicks.com
linktr.ee/jjasonhicks

To all of my bosses—
The good, the bad, and the ugly.
The petty, the craven, the selfish, and the treacherous.

You taught me more about self-preservation and self-interest than I ever could have learned on my own.

Cover art by Victor Juhasz
Cover design and interior design by the Book Cover Whisperer:
OpenBookDesign.biz

Illustrations by Victor Juhasz:
juhaszillustration.com

Names: Hicks, J. Jason, Author Title:
The War of Leadership: Hard Lessons
and Practical Truths for Surviving in
and Beyond Leadership/ J. Jason Hicks
Identifiers: LCCN 2025915343 | ISBN
978-1-960481-04-7 (paperback) |
ISBN 978-1-960481-09-2 (eBook)
Subjects: | BISAC: NON-FICTION /
Business / Leadership |
GSAFD: Business Self-Help.

LC Record available at: lccn.loc.gov/ 2025915343
Library of Congress Control Number: 2025915343

978-1-960481-04-7 Paperback
978-1-960481-09-2 eBook
978-1-960481-10-8 Audiobook

FIRST EDITION
MARCH, 2026

Politics (Business) has no relation to morals.
— **Niccolo Machiavelli**

Old age and treachery will overcome youth and hard work every time.
— **Old English proverb**

CONTENTS

INTRODUCTION i

Part I: WELCOME TO THE COLISEUM 1
   1. Unprepared for War......................... 3
   2. Unwritten Rules............................ 4
   3. New Blood 5
   4. Learn Quickly.............................. 7
   5. Tenuous State 8
   6. Expendable Resource........................ 9
   7. Inheritance 10
   8. Behind the Veil 12
   9. When in Rome 14
   10. Savior and Rival 15
   11. Ego 16
   12. No Non-Disclosures 18
   13. Integrity or Longevity...................20

Part II: NAVIGATING THE ARENA..................21
   14. You Will Be Misled 23
   15. Wager....................................24
   16. Leadership Meetings 26
   17. All Meetings Are A Stage 27
   18. Any Position 29
   19. Competent Leader 30

20. Allow Time 31
21. Parity of Information 32
22. Ownership of Ideas 33
23. Fewer People 35
24. Envy 37
25. The Language of Money 38
26. Facade 39
27. Tenure 41

Part III: HARD TRUTHS 43
28. Rules of Engagement 45
29. Success 46
30. Praise 48
31. Let Others 49
32. Befriend Everyone and No One 51
33. Deflect 53
34. No Matter What 54
35. Rewards and Results 56
36. Entrepreneur 57
37. Morals 58
38. Increases in Salary 60
39. Hierarchy 62
40. Positional Power 63
41. The One Virtue 65

Part IV: CAVEO PRINCEPS - LEADER BEWARE 67
42. The Ides of March 69

43. Nice Adversaries.................................71
44. Not a Family 72
45. Fail Fast..73
46. Fun Companies 75
47. Impossible Tasks...............................76
48. Strategic Initiatives 78
49. Too Successful.................................80
50. Open and Vulnerable 81
51. Market Turns..................................83
52. Mergers and Acquisitions.....................84
53. New Boss 86
54. Know Better 88
55. Firing En Masse 90
56. Unscrupulous 91
57. Who to Choose?..............................92
58. Flailing Leaders................................94
59. Avoidance.....................................96
60. Fewer Meetings................................97
61. Succession Planning..........................98

Part V: THE REALITY OF DISSONANCE............101
62. Aspiring Leaders.............................103
63. Conflicting Ideas 106
64. Everything You Build 107
65. Not Enough..................................108
66. Strategy and Tactics..........................110

67. Two Types of Security 112
68. Little Correlation 113
69. Ambition 115
70. The Longevity Exit 116
71. Invisible Bank Account 118
72. Scruples 120
73. Scruples II 122
74. Unseen Decisions 123
75. Sacrifice 125
76. Choose the Right 127

Part VI: THE VIRTUE OF SELF-INTEREST 129

77. The Cost of Health 131
78. Only One Arena 133
79. The Needs of the Company 134
80. Self-Interest 136
81. Entrepreneur 137
82. Noble Leaders 138
83. Going Forward 139
84. Integrity and Longevity 141

    EPILOGUE 143
    ACKNOWLEDGEMENTS 149
    AUTHOR BIO 153
    ILLUSTRATOR BIO 155
    CHAPTER/ILLUSTRATION INDEX 157

INTRODUCTION

AT FIRST, I DIDN'T UNDERSTAND WHY I WAS SO SURPRISED by the work world—why it was so different than the way I imagined it would be. Everyone seemed to be out for themselves. When I reached the leadership ranks, the mentality truly was "survival of the fittest." I didn't know why my expectations didn't line up with this reality. I didn't know where I had gotten the idea that there would be some kind of family and team-like atmosphere. And the dissonance threatened to rip me apart. It was only after many years of profound and pervasive stress that I finally remembered my first impressions of the work world.

I did not have a paper route when I was a boy. I did not mow my neighbors' lawns. I did not work at McDonald's or the local supper hall washing dishes. I did not dog sit or babysit. I did not collect empty bottles from my neighbors to return for the deposit. I had a big imagination, but I did not have the entrepreneurial gene that some kids seemed to have.

The day after my fifteenth birthday, right when I was legally able to work, my mom drove me from our idyllic suburban neighborhood. We passed sprawling fields and distant farmhouses next to old red barns and rusted silos—to a gritty inner ring city suburb of Milwaukee. The smooth white vinyl facades of my community were replaced with charcoal-stained yellow and brown brick buildings packed close together. There were few trees and rare sightings of postage-stamp patches of grass.

My oldest brother had recently married, and his bride's father owned a neighborhood grocery store. It was the typical American dream: he had been a stock boy there and then bought it on loan after the previous owner retired. I was to work there as a cashier and stock boy.

I knew very little about work. My mom disappeared to her job each day and then again at night, working any job she could get as a widowed mother of four. My father's sudden death when I was two had made things hard on all of us.

My sister had worked shifts at a movie theater at the mall before heading off to college. Both of my brothers worked at a cement plant. The two of them left in the morning, crisp and clean in jeans, T-shirts, and baseball caps. Each night, they returned home, covered in dust, their jeans coated with dots and splotches of dried cement. They would strip down to their skivvies in the laundry room, and my mother would wash their clothes right then to make ready for their six a.m. departure the following summer day.

Once, my middle brother nearly got his arm torn off, hosing out the mixing drum on a cement truck. I remember the white, cobbled emergency room bandage and sling and my brother's pale face and dissociated gaze. I also remember my mother determining right then and there that I would not be joining them at the cement plant.

I was nervous walking into the store, but I quickly settled at the sight of so many familiar faces. They had been at my brother's wedding and all the festivities leading up to and around the wedding and reception. They were not a bunch of strangers, but rather a part of a wider family. Work might be fun if you were with people you already knew, people who were already friends and family.

In our neighborhood, we were outsiders. Our father had relocated us there with his new job to a new state and a new home. The house felt even lonelier by his absence and the subsequent departures of my sister and my brother when they left for college. I had no father to mix with the other fathers in the neighborhood, and I never really fit in either. However, my first job at the store suddenly made me part of a vast extended family. My brother's wife had a sister and a brother, and they had all worked there. Her brother's wife worked there, along with her two sisters. Friends and their brothers and sisters and girlfriends, all high school or college-aged, all worked there. And, as the youngest brother of the owner's oldest daughter's new husband, I was welcomed into this sprawling network of siblings and friends and cousins and grandparents and in-laws.

I learned a lot while working at the store. About hard work. About showing up on time for a shift and punching a time clock. About hauling bales of bags up and down a flight of stairs and loading empty soda bottles from the basement to the bottling truck. About checking out customers on a busy Saturday and packing grocery bags in just the right way. I learned about family. I learned about friendship. About trust and loyalty. I learned about love and heartbreak. I learned about life.

I don't think I saw a single person get fired from that store. They all moved on to new jobs once they graduated from college. Everybody knew everybody. Everybody cared about everybody.

I hadn't thought about my time there in years, but when I looked back to try to understand the source of my dissonance, I remembered it being a wonderful, even magical time. Holidays, holiday parties, school dances, first loves, and first heartbreaks. It was a wonderful experience, a special experience. And probably the absolute *worst* experience to prepare me for the work world.

I had learned how to work, but I had not learned how to survive the War of Leadership.

— Part I —
WELCOME TO THE COLISEUM

1

Unprepared for War

One does not know what to expect when becoming a leader.

To embark on a leadership role is to step foot into a blood-soaked arena, unaware that you are a gladiator.

All the eyes upon you will know the rules. They will know what has come before you, what has befallen your predecessors, and what it takes to survive.

Much will be said about how to manage those under your charge, but little will be taught about how to navigate the leaders around you and above you.

Your vision, your expectations of this role, will not align with your experience of it.

One is never fully prepared for war.

2

Unwritten Rules

There are many unspoken and unwritten dynamics, methods, and rules to learn once you become a leader. You will be trained on none of them, but you must see them, learn them, and adapt to them quickly.

Experience will be your only guide.

> "The enemy is a very good teacher."
> — DALAI LAMA

3

New Blood

In a new leadership role, you are the new blood.

You are easy prey.

You are vulnerable.

What got you into your role will not help you in its execution.

If you cling too tightly to old skills or old people, you will not survive.

4

Learn Quickly

This is about survival.

Everyone is trying to survive.

Each failure will be hung from your neck.

Worse, your failure will reflect well on others. They did not make those mistakes. *You did*.

The longer it takes you to learn the unspoken lessons of leadership, the more vulnerable you will become.

5

Tenuous State

You may believe that you will have more security in your elevated role.

You will feel the warmth of being hired into or promoted into the leadership position.

You will be surprised to learn how little security and value you actually have.

The only person with security is the owner of the company—or their family members if you work in a family-run business, or the board members in an equity-funded business. Anyone outside those circles is expendable.

At any time, for any reason, you can be let go. Remember that.

6

Expendable Resource

You are a resource, like any other expendable thing in the company.

Resources are only used by a company in the service of saving money or making money.

In spite of any espoused mission, there is no higher aim than this. If it benefits the topmost leaders, you will be spent.

You will be consumed.

7

Inheritance

You will inherit all of the consequences and outcomes of the previous leader.

You will wonder why or how they let situations devolve to their dilapidated state. You will be able to blame your predecessor for a time. But in a short while, you will be associated with those same ills and outcomes. You will be identified as their author.

You will not be able to blame your predecessor forever. Sooner than you think, you will be under threat.

And the leaders above that former leader—who contributed to the state of your inherited area of responsibility—will happily bury you for those issues, especially when they had a hand in creating them.

8

Behind the Veil

In your new role and with each new level of leadership you reach, you will begin to see behind the veil.

Warts will be exposed to you.

Foibles of other leaders, the fragile nature of the company, the fears of others, fears within the company, the problems not widely shared or known—these unspoken realities will now be yours to keep hidden, however shocking they might be.

You will begin to hold many secrets.

9

When in Rome

A leadership team has more in common with the Roman Senate than you might think.

Gossip, undermining, jockeying for position, and outright treachery will surround you.

No one will look out for you. Do not be fooled by kind words from anyone.

You must shed your naiveté quickly if you are to survive.

10

Savior and Rival

When you assume your role, you will be welcomed as a savior while your predecessor is vilified.

Even as you are welcomed as a friend, you will be secretly viewed as a rival.

When expediency or someone else's survival dictates, you will be offered up as a scapegoat, coated in blame to deflect attention from themselves or others.

Blame is assigned more readily and easily than responsibility.

11

Ego

You have entered a den of egos.

You must learn how the ego governs and drives actions and behaviors. How it stokes insecurities.

Beware touching on those insecurities in other leaders.

No one likes to be perceived as weak or unintelligent. You will become a target.

Be equally mindful of your own ego. It will not serve you well.

12

No Non-Disclosures

There are no non-disclosure agreements in any of your conversations.

There is no confidence in your discussions or dealings. Not with your superior, not with your colleagues, and especially not with anyone in Human Resources.

Everything you say can and will be used against you.

Speak only as if your words were being broadcast over an intercom system.

13

Integrity or Longevity

After a time, you will be confronted with an ongoing choice: integrity or longevity.

You are a gladiator fighting for the promise of freedom.

You are surrounded by enemies who want to see you fail for any number of reasons, all distilling down to one thing: their own survival.

It's every man and woman for themselves.

This is management Darwinism.

This is the War of Leadership.

— Part II —
NAVIGATING THE ARENA

14

You Will Be Misled

You will be misled. You will be asked to mislead.

You will be coerced. You will be directed to coerce.

You will be deceived. You will be forced to deceive.

You will be undermined. You will be compelled to undermine.

You will be bullied. You will be driven to bully.

You will be manipulated. You will be propelled to manipulate.

You will be treated unscrupulously. You will be pressured to treat others unscrupulously.

You will learn the expectations and necessities of the War of Leadership.

15

Wager

Learn how to play poker. Risk, reward, betting, bluffing, and high stakes all mirror the kinds of informal and serious negotiations you will engage in with other leaders.

You're playing a zero-sum game.

Trust no one's words.

16

Leadership Meetings

Be mindful of the dynamics in senior leadership meetings.

Learn when to speak and when to be silent. Learn how to listen. Observe who speaks and when and how they speak. Observe when they are silent.

Watch the attitudes and behaviors of the senior-most leaders closely. Align with their energy and position.

17

All Meetings Are A Stage

Be prepared to speak in leadership meetings.
Be prepared to be asked questions you were not told to prepare for.

It is a stage and an interrogation room. It behooves others to trip you up.

Learn the art of the pause. Learn to repeat questions. Learn to respond with, "I'll get back to you on that topic."

If pressed in this way, know that an enemy has revealed themself.

18

Any Position

Any strategic or tactical position can be refuted, no matter how logical it appears to be.

Be wary of advocating too strongly for any one way, even if it is the best or right one.

There is less value in being right than you think.

If you impinge on another's ego, you will begin to see their teeth.

19

Competent Leader

Be competent without being overly competent. Here, politics serves as a guide.

Be wary of taking a bold or strong position. Be very careful if you decide to challenge anyone.

Everything you say can and *will* be used against you.

20

Allow Time

You must allow time for the senior leader to understand what you are telling them.

They have equated the success of their business with success and knowledge in all areas of the business.

If it is an area they have no expertise in, and if they have not assessed their own ego, they will see your expertise as an affront, even an attack.

21

Parity of Information

Do not make the assumption that people will draw the same conclusion when given the same information about a problem.

Each leader has their own agenda, their own battle for survival, their own fiefdoms to protect.

Right does not always make might, nor does it always mean *right*.

22

Ownership of Ideas

If you must advocate for a difficult or complicated course of action, you must allow time for those less savvy or knowledgeable to digest it.

Once your position is advocated for by others, you will see that they have negotiated with their ego, incorporated your idea, and ceased to view you as a threat, at least for the time being.

You know where the idea originally came from. That is enough.

23

Fewer People

There will be fewer people to talk with as you move up the corporate ladder.

There will be fewer people to confide in.

You will be forced to keep to yourself more.

You will find more enemies than friends.

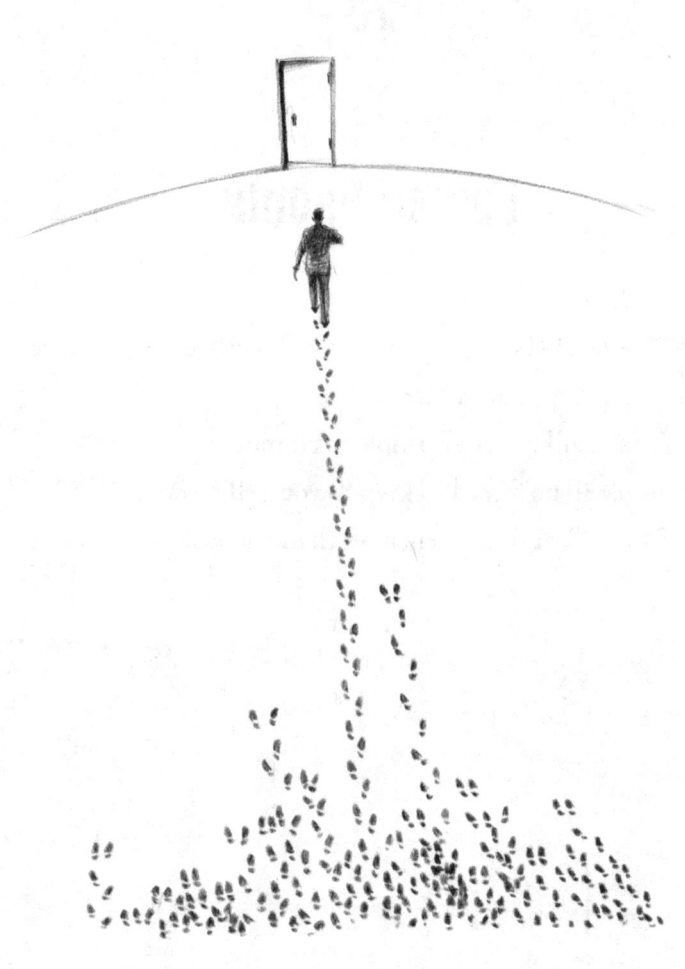

24

Envy

You must be gracious, even dismissive, regarding all attention.

Every success will generate envy in other leaders.

Leaders are always vying for a top spot in the eyes of the topmost leader. They are always scrambling for praise and attention.

If you reach a point of high praise, know that you have also become a source of envy.

25

The Language of Money

Learn the language used in place of *money*.
Revenue, profit, EBITDA, top line, net.
Money is too crude a word.
The ego does not like to be revealed so.

26

Facade

Some will be nice to you due to their nature.
Those who are exceedingly nice are afraid of your power and influence.

Everyone is just trying to survive.

27

Tenure

There is no promise of longevity. Your employment is at will.

The conditions of your employment can alter at any time for any reason. After each pay period, the slate is wiped clean.

Nothing you did before matters. Only what you do until the next pay period. Even that may not matter.

You are merely a gladiator. Your time in the arena exists in two-week increments.

— Part III —
HARD TRUTHS

28

Rules of Engagement

Do not imagine that there are rules of conduct or morality.

Only you govern your integrity.

Doing the right thing is a matter of opinion and perspective.

Be aware of holding to a code that goes against the ego—the survival instinct—of others.

29

Success

If success has a thousand fathers and failure is an orphan, then your success is a bastard.

If you outshine any other leader, including your superior, you will become a potential threat.

Shine only so brightly, but not so much that you outshine others.

30

Praise

Every leader is seeking the spotlight in one form or another, craving attention and praise from the senior-most leader.

And the senior-most leader is seeking praise from the topmost leader.

No achievements you gain will be yours alone. Do not claim them as such. Simply add them to your resume.

31

Let Others

Let others speak about your successes.
If you are good, they will be forced to acknowledge them.

Save your accomplishments for your superior, in private, when discussions of compensation or advancement arise.

Track your achievements, but don't trumpet them.

Record them on your resume, but don't promote them.

32

Befriend Everyone and No One

Befriend all of your colleagues, but trust none of them. If it is expedient to undermine you, they will.

They are trying to survive, just like you.

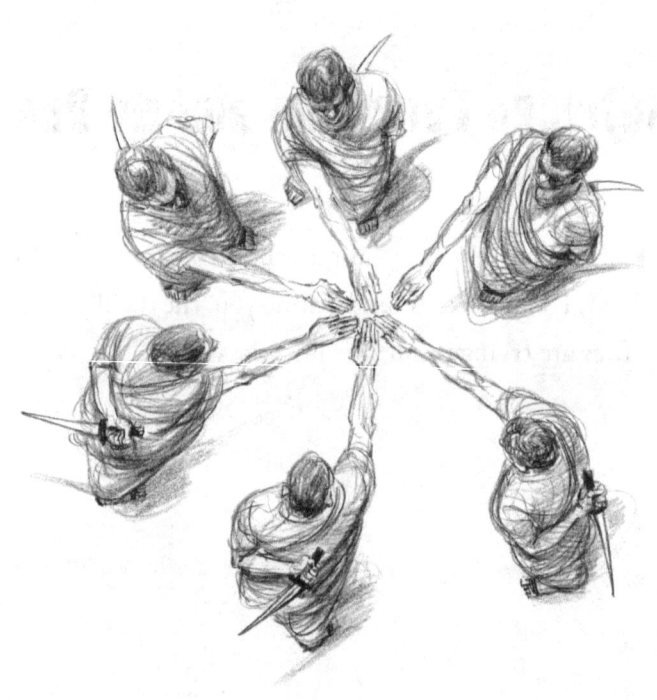

33

Deflect

You will have issues in your area of responsibility.
You must eliminate those issues as quickly as possible.
Deflect attention, directing it elsewhere by cleaning your own house quickly.

34

No Matter What

No matter the number of results or successes you achieve, you are always expendable.

You are more number than name.

You are a costly line item on the payroll ledger.

Your tenure is more tenuous than you know.

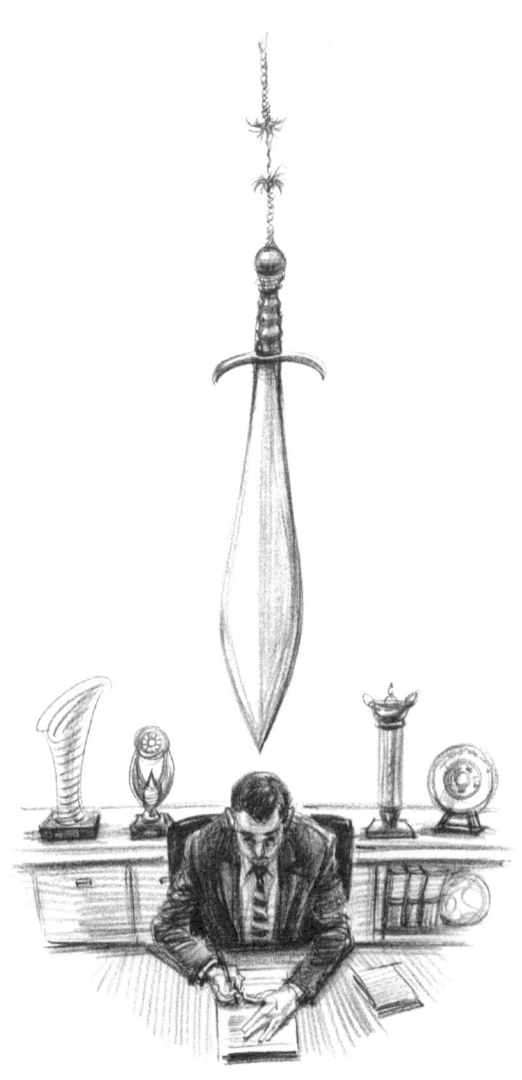

35

Rewards and Results

You will not be rewarded for doing the right thing.
You will only be rewarded for results.
It will not matter how you achieved those results.
There is no tabulation for moral conduct.

36

Entrepreneur

Be mindful when you are told to behave like an entrepreneur. This is a fallacy. This is a manipulation device designed to get you to work more, work harder.

If you do not own the thing you are working for, then you are not an entrepreneur.

You and the true entrepreneur have the same amount of time in the day, the same access to stress loads. You and the actual owner may have a similar passion for the mission of the company, but you have very different levels of investment, security, and compensation.

Here, you get all the work and none of the reward. Your wager is your mental, physical, relational, and emotional health, and you will sacrifice it all. Any return that is dangled before you will be a pittance.

You will learn the cost of longevity.

37

Morals

There are no morals in business.

When a moral decision is espoused, it is done so for another aim, another purpose: either the satisfaction of the ego or the manipulation of others. Perhaps both.

You will be surprised what leaders can live with in the name of providing for their families. You may be confronted with a similar choice.

Morality is quickly abandoned for the virtue of survival.

38

Increases in Salary

Every increase in salary makes your position more tenuous.

More salary means less security.

Be careful how hard you push for this outcome.

39

Hierarchy

Be particularly aware of the hierarchy within the leadership group.

Titles do not account for tenure, nor do they reflect affinity or familiarity with the topmost leader. Know where to express or defer your respect.

There is a pecking order. Step out of it or around it at your own peril.

40

Positional Power

Hierarchy is a powerful tool, but it must be used tacitly. The time to use the power in your role most often comes in service of an unpleasant or extremely difficult task.

41

The One Virtue

Whatever the purported aim of the company may be, there is only one true virtue it holds: make more money at all costs.

— Part IV —
CAVEO PRINCEPS - LEADER BEWARE

42

The Ides of March

History is replete with stories of leaders being betrayed. Most often, by those closest to them.

43

Nice Adversaries

Be wary of an adversary who is unexpectedly nice to you. It is very likely they have recently sought to undermine you, even betray you.

Feigned politeness can hide true intent.

Your boss might do the same thing.

You must be able to read subtle signs.

44

Not a Family

Beware of the language that seeks to cast the leadership group as a family.

You are not all in this together.

The owner is out for himself and his true family.

Everyone is out for themselves.

You will not be alone in adopting this posture.

But do not reveal it.

45

Fail Fast

The advice to "fail fast" in attempting a new process or approach is not always advisable.

You will only be lauded for your successes, not your boldness.

Every failure is a strike against you.

46

Fun Companies

Fun companies, or companies that deal in fun products, are often the darkest to work for.

The outward-marketed face rarely matches the brutal and feral environment within.

Boring companies tend to offer a more stable environment, but no more security.

47

Impossible Tasks

Beware the impossible task.

Your previous successes have prepared you for this challenge. Your ego welcomes it. But there is a great chance that you are being set up to fail.

If you succeed, an even more impossible task will be found for you.

Deflect, delay, eschew.

You must recognize what is achievable and what is not.

You must understand that you are at risk.

48

Strategic Initiatives

Be mindful if you are chosen to lead a strategic initiative that touches on a large swath of the business.

This will be presented as a great opportunity for you and your development. But here, there is no room to fail fast—or fail at all.

Senior leaders can be fickle. They have a wider view than you do. They see the tides turning before you do. They can and will pull away and leave you out on a broken limb that you thought was secure.

Convincing so many minds of a new idea, especially an idea that threatens the status quo, is dangerous for you. Top leaders have likely failed at this effort before. That's why they chose you.

The great opportunity will become an albatross. It will

appear as if you alone sought this seismic change for the business. You will be viewed with disdain. The strategy will be abandoned, and you will bear the stain of it as if you had sought it all on your own.

49

Too Successful

Beware of looking too successful or overly competent in your area of responsibility.

If you are not stressed or strained or working at all hours, your job will appear easy from the outside. You will be viewed as being overpaid. You may be viewed as lazy or complacent.

Be careful.

Senior leaders will think anyone can do what you have done.

You will be targeted for replacement—typically, by someone younger and cheaper than you.

50

Open and Vulnerable

Be cautious of advice telling you to be open and vulnerable.

Revealing yourself may expose weakness. It will lead you to let your guard down.

Familiarity will lead to contempt. And contempt will lead inevitably to treachery.

51

Market Turns

Beware of market turns or massive changes in the wider economy.

When revenues drop and profits tumble, the War of Leadership will reveal itself—even to the uninitiated.

Survival of the business and, specifically, the topmost leaders will become the foremost concern.

Everyone's security will be on the line.

Have your exit strategy ready.

52

Mergers and Acquisitions

Mergers and acquisitions are often presented as potent opportunities for the company.

The potent opportunity is to eliminate redundancy.

They do not need two of you. The new company cannot exist with two cultures.

The kinder, weaker culture will be eliminated.

53

New Boss

Beware of the new boss.

54

Know Better

Be cautious of senior leaders who believe they know more than you about your area of expertise. They are serving the edicts of their own power and their own ego.

If you oppose them or try to explain how their perception or opinion is a fallacy—or, worse, a mistake—you will have acquired a slighted enemy.

It is better to be agreeable and wrong than disagreeable and right.

55

Firing En Masse

You may be given the unsavory task of firing a lot of people at once on behalf of a senior leader as a part of a strategic effort. The act will be presented as an opportunity for you. Beware.

The savvy leader gets someone else to do so in order to keep their own hands clean. They know the stain that comes with such a thing. They know it bears an indelible black mark.

They know you will bear it for them.

Then you become a target.

The leader can then fire you to look noble and be lauded for getting rid of the person who did the heinous act.

This is a hard lesson to see coming and a hard lesson to learn.

56

Unscrupulous

Beware of the leader who asks you to do something unscrupulous on behalf of the company, however slight it may seem.

You will bear the responsibility for that act—not them.

It will be a black mark on your reputation, on your professional history—not theirs.

57

Who to Choose?

Do not assume any fealty toward you is real or permanent.

If a leader has to choose between you and their family, who do you think they will choose?

You will be surprised how quickly you can be abandoned.

58

Flailing Leaders

When other leaders lose a hold on their position or power, you will see them flail about.

They will search desperately for sympathetic ears to lessen or assuage their fears. Or they will cast aspersion in an attempt to deflect attention from themselves.

When you see this, that leader is likely already lost.

Stay away.

You cannot save them.

They will not last.

59

Avoidance

Notice when your superior or senior leaders talk with you less or avoid you altogether.

This is a sign that you are falling out of favor.

They cannot face you and their intent to fire you at the same time.

Prepare for your exit.

The trust you grant them gives them the greatest power over you.

It is a power you do not see.

60

Fewer Meetings

Beware when you are excluded from certain meetings. When you learn of discussions or potential decisions regarding your department that you were not a part of.

You were likely a component of those conversations.

Your time with the company has grown very short.

Have your exit plan close at hand.

61

Succession Planning

"Succession planning" is a euphemism for training your replacement.

Only the savviest leaders and those closest to the inner circle of the company remain in their roles. And the inner circle does not grow, does not share power.

Remember, as your success grows, your salary grows. As your salary grows, so does the attractiveness of someone younger and cheaper.

Your ambition will make you a target.

There will always be someone younger and cheaper to fill your role.

— Part V —
THE REALITY OF DISSONANCE

62

Aspiring Leaders

13 Inspiring Traits of Exceptional Leaders
By
Glenn Leibowitz[1]

13 Actual Traits of Most Leaders
By
J. Jason Hicks

1. They trust you to do the job you've been hired to do.

    1. They don't trust you. They don't trust anyone.

---

[1] Leibowitz, Glenn. "13 Inspiring Traits of Exceptional Leaders." LinkedIn. Last modified 2023. www.linkedin.com/posts/glennleibowitz_leadershipfirstquotes-entrepeneurship-leadershipdevelopment-activity-7054974901111173120-sPJa?utm_source=share&utm_medium=member_desktop&rcm=ACoAAAxQBnYBJrT9Z1uk0hYIhlvEJb1MalLUFtQ

2. They seek your advice and input.

    2. They think they know better than you. If they ask, it's just to fulfill their confirmation bias.

3. They find opportunities to let you shine.

    3. They find opportunities to set you up for failure.

4. They recognize your contributions.

    4. They take credit for your contributions.

5. They have your back during tough times.

    5. They abandon you in tough times.

6. They are master storytellers

    6. They are master manipulators.

7. They challenge you to do bigger and better things.

    7. They push you out on a limb to deflect from or take more credit for themselves.

8. They express appreciation.

    8. They withhold appreciation and give it grudgingly only when it suits some other agenda.

9. They are responsive.

   9. They are evasive.

10. They know when to apologize.

    10. They rarely apologize.

11. They give credit where credit is due.

    11. They take credit whenever possible.

12. They treat others with dignity and respect.

    12. They bully, demean, and coerce.

13. They care.

    13. They pretend to care, if they deign to pretend at all.

63

Conflicting Ideas

The world you encounter in business will differ wildly from the idealistic dreams of leadership in books and articles.

You must learn to endure cognitive dissonance if you are to survive the War of Leadership.

What you thought you saw from the outside will not be what you experience on the inside.

Your desire for authenticity will clash with the need for falsity.

Success and familiarity will breed contempt. Both will lead to failure. Higher forms of stress will lead to lower degrees of health.

Integrity will come in opposition to the desire for longevity.

64

Everything You Build

Everything you correct or build for the company is *not* yours. It never was yours.

All of your contributions belong to the company.

Any pride or ownership you feel will only serve to intensify this sense of loss.

Your achievements will be inherited and accepted by another as their own. Your name will fade more quickly than you can imagine.

Your achievements only live on your resume and in the next interview that highlights them.

65

Not Enough

You will be overburdened and overwhelmed.

You will be led to believe that you are not doing enough, not achieving enough, not giving enough.

This is a lie.

You are enough, you have been enough, you will be enough.

No one can fulfill the insatiability of the value of "more"—the only value espoused by a company.

66

Strategy and Tactics

You will be coached, coaxed, and guided to be more strategic as you grow into leadership. As you become more strategic, your work will become more internal and less external, and it will appear as if you are working less.

You will then be asked to get more tactical. To learn the details. To get into the weeds.

Then you will be critiqued for not being strategic enough. Told that you have to delegate and think of the "big picture." Told to focus on vision. To rise above.

Then it will appear again that you are not straining enough, not working enough, not struggling enough. And you will be told to get more involved in the details of the operation.

This is done to manipulate you. This is done to

reinforce the illusion that you are not doing enough and not being enough.

When you are asked to achieve things that no leader can achieve, know that you are in the War of Leadership.

67

Two Types of Security

There are only two types of security within the company: being born into the family of a family-owned business, or being so woefully underpaid and non-threatening that replacing you would be far more expensive than keeping you.

68

Little Correlation

There is surprisingly little correlation between your performance and your security.

A merger, a new boss, a failed initiative, or an error can wipe out everything you've ever done at a company.

The company retains your results, and you will be shown the door if you do not seek the door first.

69

Ambition

Ambition must be met with opportunity.

If a company does not or will not grow to provide opportunities for aspiring leaders to grow into, then those leaders will become a drag on profitability.

Success and ambition, absent opportunity, will lead to failure and attrition.

70

The Longevity Exit

While you are in the War of Leadership, you must try to preserve your job, but you must always be preparing for your untimely exit.

Maintain your contacts.

Maintain your resume.

Constantly envision your next role, your next move.

71

Invisible Bank Account

There is no invisible bank account.

Extra things you do to garner goodwill or support charity or help with a senior leader's pet project will not be tabulated.

There are no credits to be accumulated. No deposits that will add to your supposed security.

Leave time for yourself to preserve your mind and your health.

You will need both later.

72

Scruples

Some leaders choose the scruples of protecting and providing for their families over other scruples of conduct.

Only you can decide what your scruples are worth to you.

There are no morals in business, only the dictates of survival.

73

Scruples II

You do not know when, where, or how your actions, decisions, and words will extend out into the world.

While unscrupulous behavior may serve you within a company and may even be tacitly lauded, outside the company those actions and decisions might eliminate other potential opportunities.

Some networks are smaller than you think.

74

Unseen Decisions

There are many decisions you will witness but never learn the details of. You will wonder—what happened? What did that person do wrong? Why was that decision made?

If you never learn the details, you can be sure that they were made via two guiding principles: self-interest and survival.

The details are not necessary. Decisions based on these principles will be made against you as well.

75

Sacrifice

Notice when you begin to lose your temper more easily or are easily exacerbated.

Become aware of your heartbeat and the feeling of your rising blood pressure.

Notice when your sleep quality lessens or your eating habits change for the worse.

The cost of the War of Leadership will be your health.

The business will take it from you as compensation for your contributions.

No amount of sacrifice will give meaning to the business you are sacrificing for.

Longevity within the company requires the sacrifice of the longevity of your life.

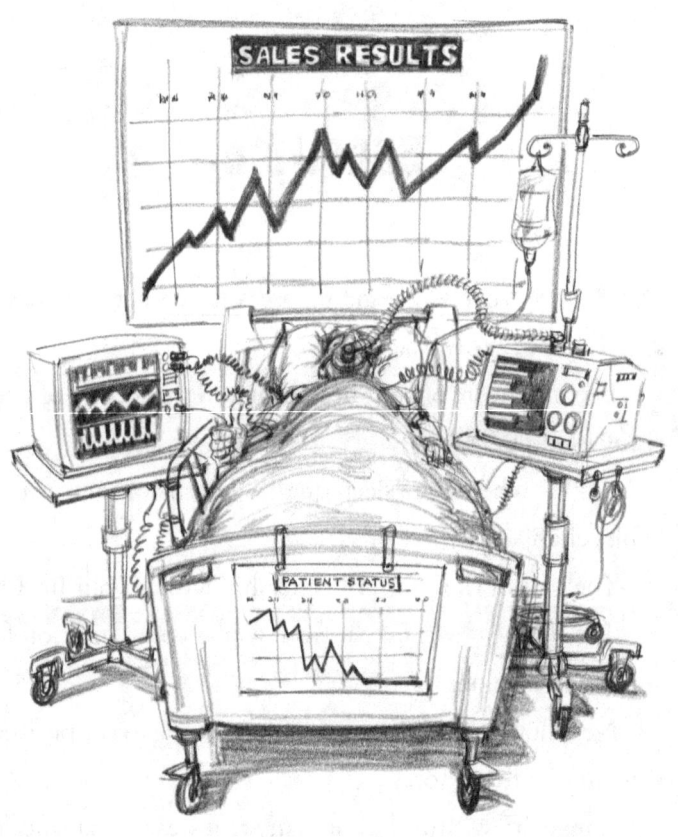

76

Choose the Right

Choosing the right thing will conflict with your desire for integrity and longevity.

The dissonance will create a strain in you that you might not notice or feel until it is too late.

The mind was not designed to hold such conflicting aims.

— Part VI —
THE VIRTUE OF SELF-INTEREST

77

The Cost of Health

You must take responsibility for your health.

You must understand what chronic stress and cortisol will do to your body and your mind.

You will think that you can endure anything, that you are strong enough to endure anything.

You might truly feel that way when you are young, but your body does keep score. It bears hidden scars that cannot be erased.

78

Only One Arena

It behooves a company to create the perception that they are the only game in town. That they are the only arena.

They will say competitors are bad and that other industries are a waste of time.

This position serves to keep you put. To make you think that you have no other options.

This is a form of manipulation to serve their self-interest. In truth, there are many arenas.

79

The Needs of the Company

You will be told to put the needs of the company before your own. Your self-interest will be presented as being in conflict with the greater good of the company. This is a fallacy and a manipulation tactic.

It asks you to sacrifice yourself when there is no sacrifice in return. No reciprocal agreement.

Remember, you are a resource to be expended.

There is no security or longevity.

You can be released at any time for any reason. Put your own needs off at your own peril.

80

Self-Interest

Self-interest does not mean selfishness.

You can still help those around you, still contribute to the success of the business, while still looking out for yourself.

The two aims are not incompatible.

81

Entrepreneur

You can be an entrepreneur—just be an entrepreneur for *you*.

Pretending to be an entrepreneur for a company within a company is a fallacy.

View your own life and career as an entrepreneurial affair.

82

Noble Leaders

There might be companies or industries with noble leaders.

They are in the small minority and are difficult to find.

If you have found one, you are lucky.

83

Going Forward

You are wise now about the War of Leadership. You know about betrayal and manipulation. You know how to recognize the ploys. You see your career and true interests as your business.

You can embark on your own in another company or in your own business. You can lead anywhere, not just in the single company you find yourself currently in. You can lead, help others, and maintain your health.

You have the ability and the power to make the choices that are right for you.

You have your own longevity to cultivate and integrity to maintain.

You have the freedom to look out for you and not sacrifice yourself for the sake of the company.

And this responsibility to yourself is as serious as a heart attack.

84

Integrity and Longevity

In the arena of the War of Leadership, there is a false choice between integrity and longevity. In fact, much of what you will encounter in the work world will come as false choices.

The reality is that you can keep your integrity and enjoy longevity in your whole life as you embark on your career.

Think beyond the arena you have found yourself in. There is so much outside of the company. There is so much more to your life.

EPILOGUE

As I reflected on my time as a leader, I realized that much of the internal dissonance and strain I had experienced came from an unconscious search. Without realizing it, I had wanted to replicate that first work environment at that neighborhood grocery store. Company cultures that appealed to me were always the friends and family atmosphere. Not the stated tenets or rubric of the company's culture and mission—though I often thought that those things were code for that feeling. If it drew everyone together just like the store did, it drew me in as well.

Do you remember what you were searching for in the first job you had? What needs were you looking to meet in those jobs, with those companies?

Several times throughout my career, I tried to recreate that environment. In the end, it always fell flat or got taken away. To be sure, I experienced moments of it. I was able to create instances when I had control and could recreate it to some extent. But the leaders above me opted for the pressure cooker of higher productivity to serve their compulsive need for *more*.

Another component in my personal makeup that I wasn't fully aware of at that time both did and didn't prepare me for the work world: I grew up with a Midwest work ethic. Through their words and examples, my family taught me to work hard and keep working hard no matter what. I did not know that my work ethic would make me vulnerable to exploitation.

Are you sacrificing something for work that you might one day regret? Is there something in your makeup that makes it easier to take advantage of you?

If I had held a wider view of my life and had seen my career as my own entrepreneurial business, I would not have passed up opportunities to learn and grow for my own benefit. I would not have sacrificed my time to the company. Instead, I spent years choosing the greater good of the company. Yet no one in the companies I worked for remembers the holidays and family gatherings I missed for projects that no longer matter. Only I know what I sacrificed and lost in the name of working hard.

What choices are you making?

If I had known what I was doing to myself, I would have taken a more active interest in my health and well-being. I would have been mindful of my longevity and not spent my time so cavalierly. As it turned out, I had to recover from years of unhealthy behaviors and the effects of chronic stress. I began asking questions of my professional life and about the assumptions that drove me. I spent years doing deep soul work. I learned that I had lost myself, but I didn't know where to look to find myself.

Have you forgotten your dreams? Do you feel like you've surrendered them or lost them altogether?

My break with work came after an unexpected termination from a company I loved. After a year in the wilderness, I began to think about this book—and others. And then I remembered my first love, even before I had the job at the grocery store. My first dreams were of writing, and I decided to apply myself to those dreams. I figured it was at least as important as the job I worked at to pay the bills. And I went on to write three books, with more to come.

What passion have you hidden from in favor of the "needs" of your job?

Eventually, I was able to see my life as more than my

career. A career that I had become successful in but that I hadn't chosen. I had essentially fallen into it through aptitude, competence, and hard work. It wasn't even close to my dream.

Are you really good or even great at work that you don't enjoy or that you perhaps even hate?

I was able to have a healthier approach to jobs going forward when I learned to integrate my creative work as well. Writing showed me a different way forward. Paying attention to my health made me mindful of my longevity. I wanted more life for myself, not solely for the benefit of the company. To do that, I had to let go of the hard lessons and truths I lived through in the arena of work. The War of Leadership is a distillation of those lessons.

Are you ready to let go of what you've been conditioned to be in order to become who you really are?

Ultimately, I learned that I was hopelessly naive. I was as naive as that boy who showed up for his first day of work. The boy who knew he had to work as hard as his brothers, sister, and mother did. But I had been unprepared for the arena. No place was ever like that grocery store again. I survived what followed, not unscathed, but free to create the life that I dreamed of. You can too.

EPILOGUE

I have received many calls from colleagues who were suddenly terminated from jobs that they felt secure in. Each time, I have done my best to help them see a life beyond their arena. To know that the battle is not for the next job or the next raise or the next promotion. The battle is for your life and your dreams.

I hope that these hard lessons and practical truths can save you the years I spent learning them. I hope you know that you can be a successful leader without surrendering your integrity. I hope you believe that your life is bigger than your career. I hope you see that now is the time. That your life is the arena. Fight for your dreams. Fight as if your life depends on it. It most certainly does.

ACKNOWLEDGEMENTS

Thank you to John Heider's *The Tao of Leadership* and Steven Pressfield's *The War of Art* for the inspiration for this book and the mashup of the title, and thank you to Lao Tzu of course.

Thank you to Brannan Sirratt for her expertise in helping me organize and clarify this book from the loose conglomeration of pages and ideas into the book you now hold.

It was a pleasure to work with Victor Juhasz on the illustrations for this book. I would say that it was a dream come true, except for the fact that I never dreamed that such a thing was even possible for me. His sensibilities of classical sources and whimsy gave this book the lightness it needed. Thanks, Vic!

Thank you to Jennifer Hicks for copy editing *The War of Leadership* and getting it ready for Christine at Open Book Design for interior design.

I am hopeful that this book provides the necessary wisdom to help those embarking on the leadership path who perhaps have the same kind of naivete I brought to the work world. It is never too late to refocus your goals beyond the work world to the wider arena of your life and your dreams.

Please take a few moments to leave a review. Authors rely heavily on reviews to increase the chances that new readers will learn about books they may enjoy. Thank you!

Connect with Jason on Instagram, Facebook, and his website.

You may access all of the above information and more via my Linktree and this QR code:

No generative artificial intelligence (AI) was used in the writing of this work or cover art. The author reserves the rights for this work and cover art, which cannot be reproduced and/or otherwise used in any manner. The author expressly prohibits any entity from using this publication for purposes of training AI technologies to generate text or artwork, including, without limitation, technologies that are capable of generating works in the same style or genre as this publication.

AUTHOR BIO

J. JASON HICKS STUDIED English Literature, Political Science, and World Religions, with a focus on classic literature, at the University of Wisconsin Oshkosh. He is the author of The Annals of the Last Emissary fantasy series. *The War of Leadership* is his first nonfiction novel. He lives in Tucson, Arizona with his wife and his dog Maya.

www.jjasonhicks.com
linktr.ee/jjasonhicks

ILLUSTRATOR BIO

FOR MORE THAN FIFTY YEARS, Victor Juhasz has created illustrations for countless national magazines, newspapers, and periodicals. He has also served as a courtroom artist and as an embedded artist, drawing illustrations of many soldiers and marines both here and abroad. He has illustrated several children's books and books by bestselling authors. He lives in the New York Berkshires with his wife, Terri Cole, psychotherapist, author, instructor, and speaker. They have three sons. seven grandchildren, eight hens, one rooster, two geese, and a pit mix pooch named Charli.

www.juhaszillustration.com

CHAPTER/ILLUSTRATION INDEX

Cover: The Needs of the Company

Part I: Welcome to the Coliseum
        Illustration: [New] New Blood

1. Unprepared for War
2. Unwritten Rules
3. New Blood
   Illustration: The Fool
4. Learn Quickly
5. Tenuous State
6. Expendable Resource
7. Inheritance
   Illustration: Inheritance
8. Behind the Veil
   Illustration: Behind the Veil
9. When in Rome
10. Savior and Rival

11. Ego
   Illustration: Ego

12. No Non-Disclosures
    Illustration: Competent Leader

13. Integrity or Longevity

Part II: Navigating the Arena
   Illustration: Den of Lions

14. You will be misled

15. Wager
    Illustration: Wager

16. Leadership Meetings

17. All Meetings are a Stage
    Illustration: All Meetings are a Stage

18. Any Position

19. Competent Leader

20. Allow Time

21. Parity of Information

22. Ownership of Ideas
    Illustration: Ownership of Ideas

23. Fewer People
    Illustration: Fewer People

24. Envy

25. The Language of Money
26. Façade
   Illustration: Façade
27. Tenure

Part III: Hard Truths
   Illustration: Little Correlation

28. Rules of Engagement
29. Success
   Illustration: Success
30. Praise
31. Let Others
   Illustration: Let Others
32. Befriend Everyone and No One
   Illustration: Befriend Everyone and No One
33. Deflect
34. No Matter What
   Illustration: No Matter What
35. Rewards and Results
36. Entrepreneur
37. Morals
   Illustration: Morals

38. Increases in Salary
   Illustration: Increase in Salary

39. Hierarchy

40. Positional Power
    Illustration: Positional Power

41. The One Virtue

Part IV: Caveo Princeps – Leader Beware
   Illustration: Nice Adversaries

42. The Ides of March
    Illustration: The Ides of March

43. Nice Adversaries

44. Not a Family

45. Fail Fast
    Illustration: Fail Fast

46. Fun Companies

47. Impossible Tasks
    Illustration: Strategy and Tactics

48. Strategic Initiatives

49. Too Successful

50. Open and Vulnerable
    Illustration: Open and Vulnerable

51. Market Turn
52. Mergers and Acquisitions
    Illustration: Mergers and Acquisitions
53. New Boss
    Illustration: Tenure
54. Know Better
    Illustration: Know Better
55. Firing En Masse
56. Unscrupulous
57. Who to Choose
    Illustration: Who to Choose
58. Flailing Leaders
    Illustration: Flailing Leaders
59. Avoidance
60. Fewer Meetings
61. Succession Planning
    Illustration: Succession Planning

Part V: The Reality of Dissonance
    Illustration: Everything You Build

62. Aspiring Leaders
63. Conflicting Ideas

64. Everything You Build

65. Not Enough
    Illustration: Hierarchy

66. Strategy and Tactics

67. Two Types of Security

68. Little Correlation
    Illustration: Tenuous State

69. Ambition

70. The Longevity Exit
    Illustration: Market Turns

71. Invisible Bank Account
    Illustration: Invisible Bank Account

72. Scruples
    Illustration: Scruples

73. Scruples II

74. Unseen Decisions
    Illustration: Unseen Decisions

75. Sacrifice
    Illustration: Sacrifice

76. Choose the Right

Part VI: The Virtue of Self-Interest
        Illustration: Self-Interest

77. The Cost of Health
   Illustration: The Cost of Health

78. Only One Arena

79. The Needs of the Company
   Illustration: The Needs of the Company

80. Self-Interest

81. Entrepreneur

82. Noble Leaders

83. Going Forward

84. Integrity and Longevity
   Illustration: Integrity and Longevity

   Illustration: Envy

www.ingramcontent.com/pod-product-compliance
Lightning Source LLC
LaVergne TN
LVHW032010070526
838202LV00059B/6375